THE
BIG
ENCYCLOPEDIA
OF DEFUNCT
ANIMALS

VOLUME VII

STANTON F. FINK

Acknowledgments

and Dedication

To my father, in whose books I discovered my first monsters.

To Nikolas Draper-Ivey, he who wields the sword of Ragnarok, and who has been awarded the Decorations of Omega; he who stands tall to cleave open the Heavens.

To Mariano Silvera, who should have had his own artbooks

To Doctor David Morafka, who helped teach me to be more picky with my information.

To my friends, who helped push me to make this.

Table of Contents

Introduction

The purpose of this coloring book series is to provide information on various prehistoric animals both profoundly famous and incredibly obscure to artists of all ages. Of course, there is a lot of material to work with, as animals have been a major component of Earth's ecosystems for at least 670 million years.

For the sake of space and workability, each volume will contain 17 entries: ideally, one species for each geological time period, if possible. If you, or your inner and or outer child do not see your favorite prehistoric animal here, it may be eventually featured in another volume. Or, contact me at apokryltaros@gmail.com to have it put into a later volume.

Glossary

- **Aquatic**- Living in water.
- **Arthropod**- Any member of the animal phylum Arthropoda, including trilobites, arachnids, crustaceans, insects, myriapods and their relatives. All arthropods have armor-like, jointed exoskeletons made of chitin-derived plates, sometimes reinforced with calcium carbonate, and jointed limbs.
- **Cambrian**- A period of time in the Paleozoic Era from 541 to 485 million years ago.
- **Carboniferous**- A period of time in the Paleozoic Era from 359 to 300 million years ago.
- **Cenozoic**- An era of time in the Phanerozoic Eon from 65 million years ago until now.
- **Chordate**- Any member of the animal phylum Chordata, including sea squirts, lancet fish, and vertebrates (such as lampreys, sharks, tuna, frogs, lizards, chickens, and people). All chordates have, at least at some point in their life cycle, a notochord, a long, flexible rod, usually made of cartilage, or, in the case of most vertebrates, cartilage and bone, running down the back from head to tail, directly beneath the neural tube.
- **Cnidarian**- Any member of the animal phylum Cnidaria, such as jellyfish, box jellies, Portuguese Man'o'war, sea anemones, coral and the parasitic myxozoans. Cnidarians are usually radially symmetrical, and have unique, venom-injecting stinging cells called "cnidocytes."
- **Cretaceous**- The last period of time in the Mesozoic Era, from 144 to 66 million years ago.
- **Devonian-** A period of time in the Paleozoic Era from 414 to 360 million years ago.
- **Ediacaran-** The last period of time in the Precambrian Eon from 635 to 542 million years ago.
- **Eocene**- A period of time in the Cenozoic Era from 55 to 33 million years ago.
- **Fauna**- In an ecological context, "fauna" refers to the animal components of an ecosystem.
- **Formation**- In a geological or paleontological context, a formation is a group of rock layers.
- **Gnathostome**- A gnathostome is any vertebrate chordate with a moveable jaw (or had an ancestor with one).
- **Holocene**- A period of time in the Cenozoic Era from 12,000 years ago until now.
- ***Incertae sedis*-** A Latin phrase literally meaning "uncertain seat." *"Incertae sedis"* is a term in classification used to refer to a species or group whose relationships with related organisms are unclear or poorly defined.
- **Jurassic**- The second period of time in the Mesozoic Era, from 199 to 145 million years ago.
- **Mesozoic**- An era of time in the Phanerozoic Eon from 249 to 66 million years ago.
- **Miocene**- A period of time in the Cenozoic Era from 23 to 5 million years ago.

- **Mollusk**- Any member of the animal phylum Mollusca, including snails, clams, squid, octopuses, tusk shells and chitons. Most mollusks have a calcium carbonate shell, and a toothed, file-like tongue called a radula. All mollusks have a cape-like organ, the mantle, which usually secretes the shell, and houses breathing organs, and a nervous system.
- **Nekton**- Any aquatic animal that lives either entirely or almost entirely in the water column, and relies on its own swimming or propulsion abilities to keep and move itself in and around the water column. Anchovies, porpoises and ichthyosaurs are examples of nekton.
- **Neogene**- The second third of the Cenozoic Era, comprising of the Miocene and the Pliocene periods.
- **Oligocene**- A period of time in the Cenozoic Era from 33 to 23 million years ago.
- **Ordovician**- A period of time in the Paleozoic Era from 484 to 440 million years ago.
- **Paleocene**- A period of time in the Cenozoic Era from 65 to 55 million years ago.
- **Paleogene**- The first third of the Cenozoic Era, comprising of the Paleocene, Eocene, and Oligocene.
- **Paleozoic**- An era of time in the Phanerozoic Eon from 249 to 66 million years ago.
- **Permian**- The last period of time in the Paleozoic Era, the time of "The Great Dying," or most severe of all known extinction events, from 299 to 250 million years ago.
- **Pharynx**- A structure in the throat of many animals located directly behind the mouth or oral chamber. In vertebrates, it often houses breathing structures, like gills.
- **Plankton**- An organism that uses water currents and waterflow to as its primary means of transportation in the water column because it is either too small to move long distances by its own power, or lacks the ability to propel itself entirely. Sargassum seaweed and jellyfish are two varieties of plankton.
- **Pleistocene**- A period of time in the Cenozoic Era from 3 million years ago until 12 thousand years ago.
- **Pliocene**- A period of time in the Cenozoic Era from 5 to 3 million years ago.
- **Quaternary**- The last third of the Cenozoic Era, comprising of the Pleistocene and the Holocene periods.
- **Terrestrial**- Living on land.
- **Triassic**- The first period of time in the Mesozoic Era, from 249 to 200 million years ago.

Name	*Namacalathus hermanastes*
Phylum	*incertae sedis*
Size	Stalk up to 30 millimeters high, and 1 to 2 millimeters in diameter. Cup 2 to 25 millimeters in diameter, height of cup 0.7 to 1.3 millimeters.
Time Period	Late Ediacaran, 549 to 542 million years ago.
Location	*Cloudina* formations in Canada, Namibia, Oman, Paraguay, Siberia
Comments	*Namacalathus hermanastes* is one of the earliest known shell-forming animals. Its unique winecup-like fossils are always found in association with mounds of *Cloudina* shells, (the tuba-shaped shells in the picture) another important Precambrian shell-forming organism. These *Cloudina* formations where *Namacalathus* is found occur in five separate localities in Canada, Namibia (in the Nama Formation where it was first found and originally named for), Oman, Paraguay, and Siberia.

What animal phylum *N. hermanastes* belongs to remains debatable. When its fossils were first discovered, the cups were thought to have been made by polyps similar to those of cnidarians, especially since the creatures apparently could replicate by budding off of each other. More comprehensive examinations of the walls of the cups, and of the cups' architecture, like how no known cup-producing cnidarians have ever produced a cup with windows, now hint that the cups' builders may have been more complex animals, possibly related to lophophorates similar or ancestral to the bryozoans or brachiopods.

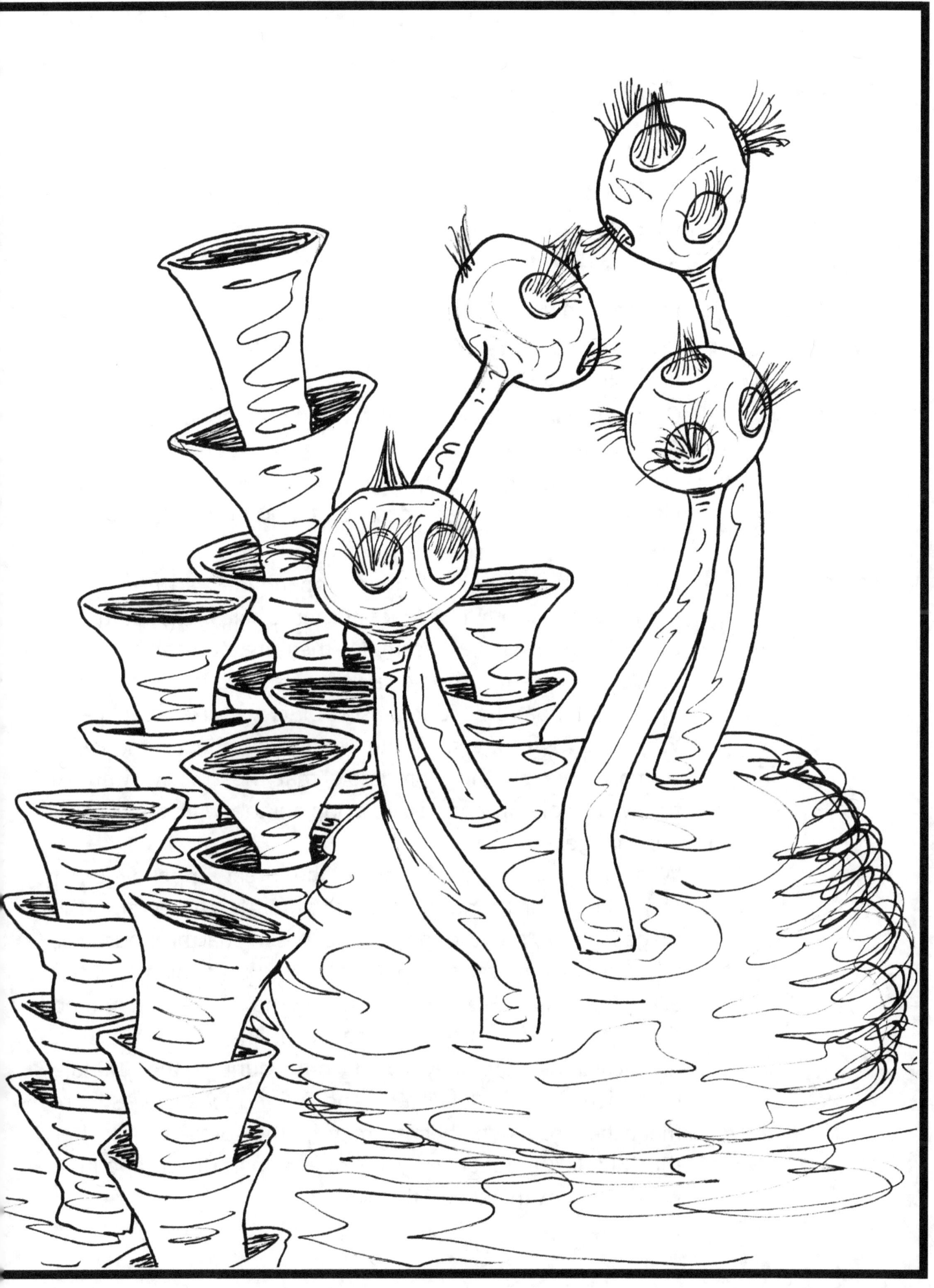

Name	*Forfexicaris valida*
Phylum	Arthropoda
clade	Arachnomorpha
Class	Megacheira
Order	Pectocaridida
Family	Forfexicarididae
Size	Bivalved carapace about 15 millimeters long and 13 millimeters high.
Time Period	Qiongzhusian or "Stage 3" of the Early Cambrian, about 518 million years ago.
Location	Holotype found in the Xiaolantian section of the Maotianshan Shales, 2nd specimen found in the Maotianshan section.
Comments	*Forfexicaris valida* is a "great appendage" arthropod, or megacheiran, from the Maotianshan Shales Lagerstätte or Chengjiang Biota, that resembles the unrelated ostracods. *F. valida* has its entire body, save for its eyes, antennae, and "great appendages," hidden inside of its egg-like carapace.

While the fossils are similar in size to lentil beans, the living animals were probably predators that most likely swam in the water column and seized zooplankton with their "great appendages."

While, or or perhaps because, the great appendage, or megacheiran arthropods resemble primitive chelicerates, the megacheirans are thought to be basal euarthropods (i.e., relatives of crustaceans, chelicerates and uniramians). If the Silurian-aged *Enalikter,* and the Devonian-aged *Bundenbachiellus* are not megacheirans, then the last megacheirans probably died out during the Middle Cambrian. If *Enalikter* and *Bundenbachiellus* are megacheirans, then their scarcity in the fossil record after the Middle Cambrian may be due in part to competition with more advanced euarthropods.

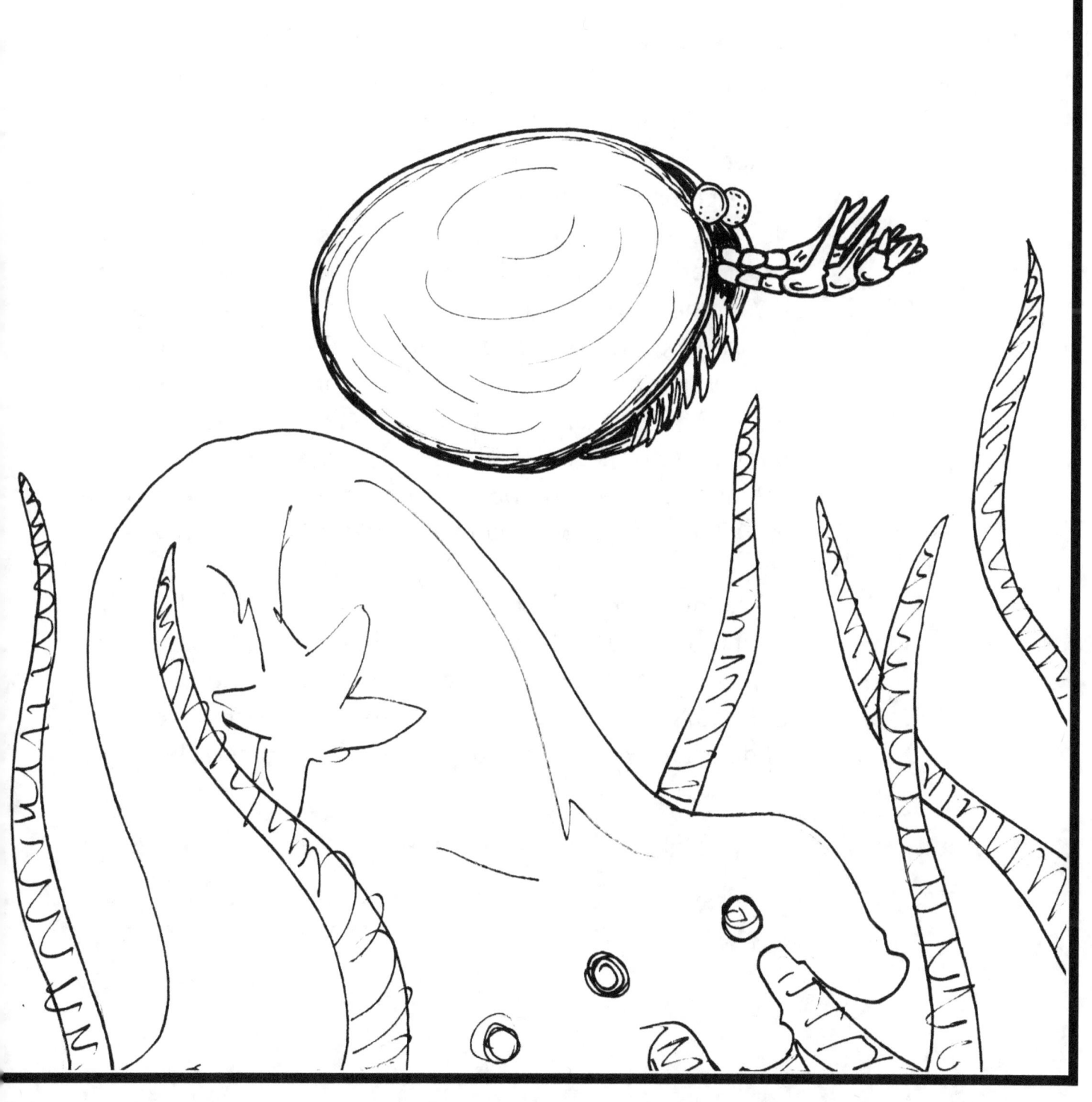

Name	*Bolboporites uncinatus*
Phylum	Echinodermata
Class	Eocrinoidea
Family	Bolboporitidae
Size	Theca (body) up to 15 millimeters in diameter.
Time Period	The Darriwllian Epoch, Middle Ordovician period, 469 to 463 million years ago.
Location	Estonia, Latvia, Saint Petersburg area of Russia.
Comments	The Ordovician-aged calcite cones named *"Bolboporites"* from the Baltic Sea are now thought to be a group of cone-shaped, single-armed eocrinoid echinoderms. When these honeycombed fossils were originally discovered, they were described by H. C. Pander in 1830 as being some sort of small, odd "horn coral." In 1955, a Russian researcher, A.Yeltysheva, restored *Bolboporites* as a "horned" starfish similar to to the knobbed starfish of *Protoreaster*, under the assumption that the fossils were of echinoderm "horns."

In 1994, Russian researchers Rozhnov and Kushlina reinterpreted these "horns" as the thecae of eocrinoids, with the apex of the cone buried in mud, and the "base" being the oral surface, with various divots corresponding to the socket of a single arm, mouth, and madreporite.

The genus is thought to have originated in the Baltic region during the Middle Ordovician, with at least six species. The genus would eventually spread into North America, with *B. uncinata*'s sister species, *B. americana*, being found in Middle Ordovician strata of Quebec, Ontario and New York.

Name	*Nerepisacanthus denisoni*
Phylum	Chordata
Class	Acanthodii
Order	Ischnacanthiformes
Family	Acritolepidae
Size	Complete specimen from the Bertie Formation about 10 centimeters in length; the incomplete Cunningham Creek specimens suggest adult lengths of up to 20 centimeters.
Time Period	From the Telychelian Stage until Ludfordian Stage, Middle Silurian period, 436 to 428 million years ago.
Location	Cunningham Creek Formation, New Brunswick, Canada, and Bertie Formation Konservat-Lagerstätte, Ontario, Canada.
Comments	*Nerepisacanthus denisoni* is a medium-sized, marine acanthodian fish from Middle Silurian Canada. It is, so far, the only Silurian-aged acanthodian known from articulated fossils: the Cunningham Creek specimens being incomplete, and the Bertie Formation specimen being complete.
	Its small, but sharp teeth strongly suggest it was a predator, probably seizing smaller fishes similar to its Devonian relative, *Ischnacanthus*.
	The anatomy of the fossils, especially of the Bertie Formation specimen, show that acanthodians are closely related to the cartilaginous fishes, either by being very closely related to very primitive cartilaginous fishes, or by showing that the acanthodians are, themselves, a subgroup within Chondrichthyes.

Name	*Medusaster rhenanus*
Phylum	Echinodermata
Class	Ophiuroidea
Order	Stenurida
Family	Palaeuridae
Size	Largest known specimens body and arm up to aboutl, at very most, 10 centimeters in diameter.
Time Period	Emsian epoch of the Early Devonian period, 407 to 393 million years ago
Location	Gemünden municipality, Rhein-Hunsrück, Germany
Comments	*Medusaster rhenanus* is an unusual (albeit very small) brittlestar from the Early Devonian Hunsrück Lagerstätte in Germany. It is unusual in that individuals had anywhere from 10 to 16 arms. Individuals of *Medusaster* also had large, robust bodydiscs, and (granted, not visible in the picture) very large, wide mouths.

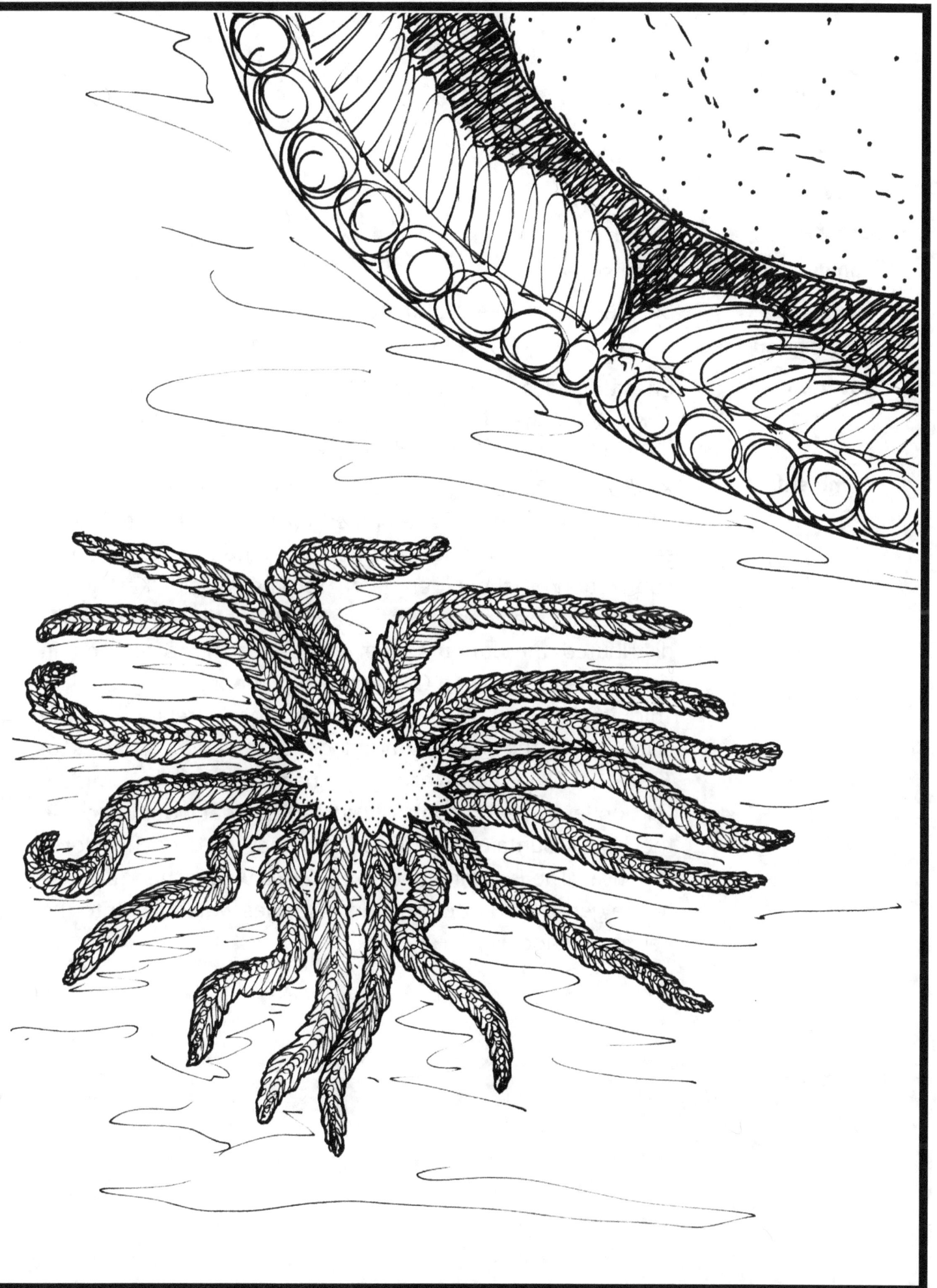

Name

Kaskia chesterensis

Phylum   Arthropoda

Class   Trilobita

Order   Proetida

Family   Phillipsiidae

Size   Bodylength up to 4 centimeters.

Time Period Upper Mississippian of the Middle Carboniferous

Location   Chester series of southern Illinois and western Kentucky, Pitkin and Mayes formations in northeastern Oklahoma, and the Maxville limestone of Pennsylvania.

Comments   *Kaskia chesterensis* is a Middle Carboniferous-aged phillipsiid proetid trilobite named for the Chester geological series: in addition to its specific name, the genus name is a contraction of the older name for the series, "Kaskaskia." This species was named so because its fossils are plentifully distributed throughout all of the series' horizons, and in similar marine strata in Oklahoma and Pennsylvania.

Trilobites of the genus *Kaskia* are closely related to the trilobites of the similarly-aged genus *Paladin*. Species of *Kaskia* thrived in North America during the Middle Carboniferous, and eventually spread to what would become the Ural Mountains in Russia after they died out in North America. The Russian species of *Kaskia* would then give rise to the genus *Ditomopyge*, whose species would last into the Permian Period.

Name	*Sinohelicoprion changhsingensis*
Phylum	Chordata
Class	Chondrichthyes
Subclass	Holocephali
Order	Eugeneodontida
Family	Helicoprionidae
Size	Largest portion of toothwhorl about 12 centimeters long. Living animal may have been as large as a modern dogfish.
Time Period	Changhsingian Stage of the Late Permian, 254 to 252 million years ago.
Location	Changxing Formation, Changxing, Zhejiang Province, China.
Comments	*Sinohelicoprion changhsingensis* is an extinct species of holocephalan cartilaginous fish from the Late Permian of Zhejiang Province, China. As its genus name suggests, *S. changhsingensis* was named after the better known *Helicoprion* (the head of the larger animal in the picture), as the holotype teeth were originally compared to those of the latter. When larger portions of the toothwhorl were found, researchers would then notice greater similarities between *Sinohelicoprion* and another helicoprionid genus, *Helicampodus*.

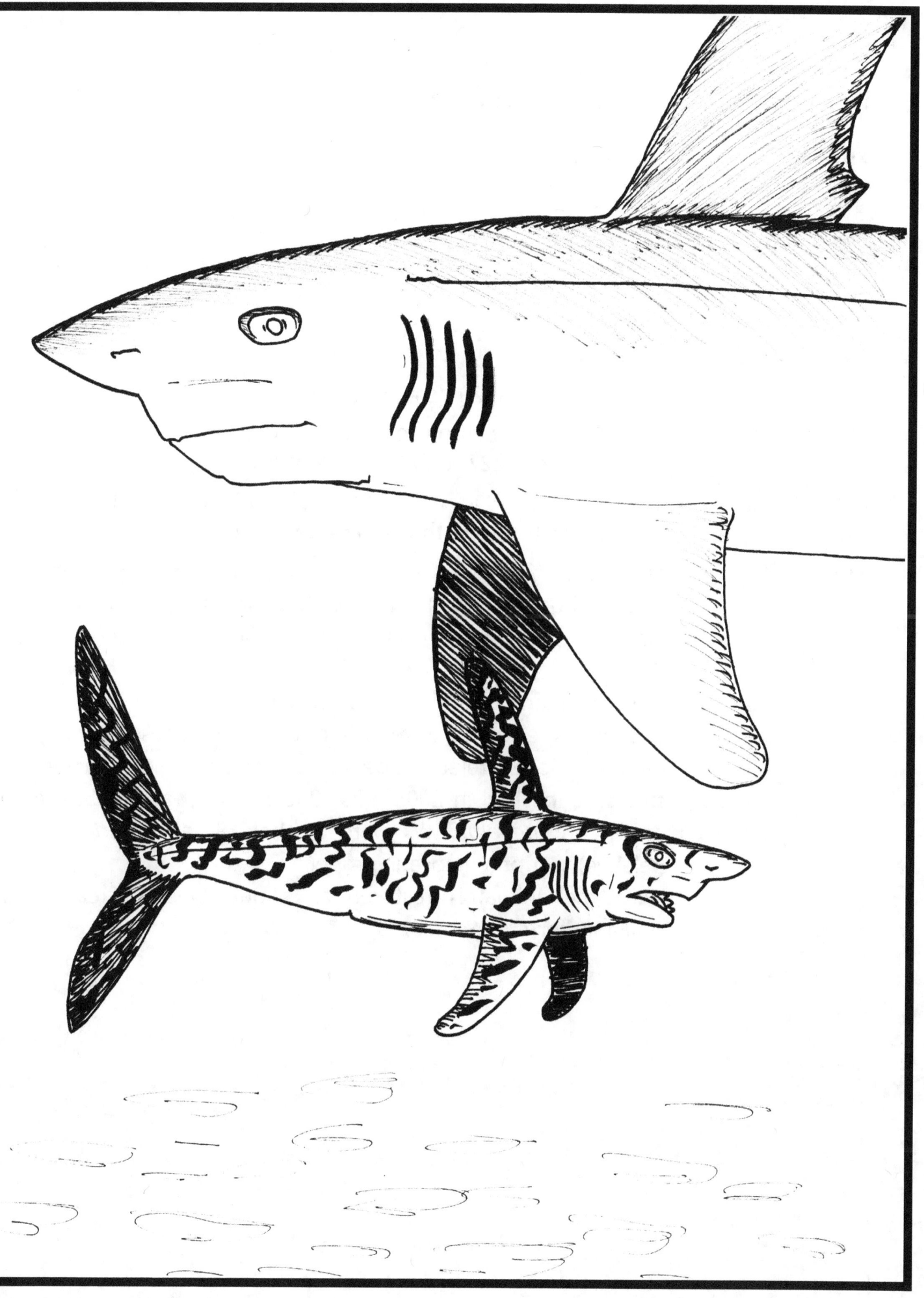

Name

Eucoelophysis baldwini

Phylum	Chordata
Class	Reptilia
clade	Archosauria
clade	Dinosauriformes
clade	Dracohors
Family	Silesauridae
Size	Pubis bone up to 20 centimeters long
Time Period	Revueltian faunachron of the Early Norian Epoch, Late Triassic Period, 227 to 225 million years ago.
Location	Cross quarry on Orphan Mesa, Petrified Forest Formation of the Chinle Group, north-central New Mexico.
Comments	*Eucoelophysis baldwini* is a species of silesaurid dinosauriform from Late Triassic New Mexico. *Eucoelophysis* (and other members of the family Silesauridae) is not a dinosaur *per se*, but is related to the common ancestor of saurischian and ornithischian dinosaurs.

The first specimens were thought to be bones of the a dinosaur closely related *Coelophysis*, but, two independent studies published in 2005 and 2006 demonstrated that the bones of *Eucoelophysis* were neither of (a) *Coelophysis* (relative), nor of a dinosaur, proper.

Here, the animal is restored as a quadrupedal creature similar in form to *Silesaurus*.

Name	*Zigzagiceras zigzag*
Phylum	Mollusca
Class	Cephalopoda
Subclass	Ammonoidea
Order	Ammonitida
Family	Perisphinctidae
Size	Adult shell up to 7 centimeters in diameter, 2 centimeters wide.
Time Period	Bathonian Epoch of the Middle Jurassic Period, about 168 to 167 million years ago.
Location	Zig Zag Quarry, Zig Zag Hill, near Dorset, England. Also la Nièvre, France, and Catalan Basin, Spain.
Comments	*Zigzagiceras zigzag* is a Middle Jurassic ammonoid known from Dorset, England, la Nièvre, France and Spain. It is named both after Zig Zag Hill, which is infamous for its dangerous, difficult to navigate roads, and for the labyrinthinely complex architecture of its internal chambers. The living animals may have lived in coastal shallows, and lagoons.
	Several other species are found in other Middle Jurassic marine strata throughout Europe and Russia.

Name	*Halszkaraptor escuilliei*
Phylum	Chordata
clade	Archosauria
clade	Dinosauria
Order	Saurischia
Suborder	Theropoda
Family	Dromeosauridae
Subfamily	Halszkaraptorinae
Size	Bodylength with head and tail extended about 90 centimeters.
Time Period	Campanian Epoch of the Late Cretaceous, about 75 to 71 million years ago.
Location	Probably the Bayn Dzak member of the Djadochta Formation, Ukhaa Tolgod, Southern Mongolia.
Comments	At an unknown date, fossil poachers illegally excavated the fossil of a duck-sized, subadult dromeosaur from what is assumed to be the Djadochta Formation in Mongolia. Then it would pass through the hands of several fossil dealers until it fell into the clutches of François Escuillié, who, upon realizing it was an undescribed species, took it to the Royal Belgian Institute of Natural Sciences in Brussels, Belgium, for authentification, eventually via X-rays. Soon after, Escuillié was convinced to return the fossil, named *Halszkaraptor escuilliei*, after Halszka Osmólska, a late Polish specialist of Mongolian dinosaurs, and himself, to the Mongolian government.
	Analyses of the bone chemistry suggest the animal had a semi-aquatic lifestyle. Features of its skeletons support this, as it was apparently able to swim using its strong hindlegs to kick or paddle, in addition to wade about. Its forelegs could flap like flippers. It could use its small, but sharp teeth to seize small fish. Presumedly, *Halszkaraptor* was able to walk freely about on land as the female, like all other female dinosaurs (avian and nonavian), had to come ashore to lay eggs.

Name	*Triisodon quivirensis*
Phylum	Chordata
Class	Mammalia
Order	Mesonychia
Family	Triisodontidae
Size	Skull and skeletal material suggest a robustly built, wolf-sized animal.
Time Period	Torrejonian Stage of the Paleocene Period, 63 to 58 million years ago
Location	San Juan Basin, New Mexico
Comments	*Triisodon quivirensis* is an extinct mesonychian mammal from the Paleocene of New Mexico. This wolf-sized animal was probably carnivorous, and wear on its teeth suggest it crunched bone. The genus is named for a unique carnassial tooth with three prominent cusps modified into three massive prongs. The cat-sized triisodontid, *Eoconodon*, also from Paleocene New Mexico, is closely related. The Chinese-Mongolian Eocene triisodontid,*Paratriisodon*, is known from very large teeth, and may or may not be of the carnivorous artiodactyl *Andrewsarchus*.

The triisodontids are thought to be ancestral to the mesonychians of Mesonychidae and Hapalodectidae, as the triisodontids have very similar, but more simpler-shaped teeth. Triisodontids may have been driven into extinction due to competition with species of Mesonychidae.

Name	*Boavus occidentalis*
Phylum	Chordata
Class	Reptilia
Order	Squamata
Suborder	Serpentes
Family	Boiidae
Size	Complete specimens range in length from 6 to 8 feet, comparible to *Boa constrictor*.
Time Period	Bridgerian land stage of the Early Eocene until the Orellan land stage of the Early Oligocene, 50 to 33 million years ago
Location	Eocene localities include the Grizzly Buttes, near Fort Bridger, Wyoming, and the Green River Shales Lagerstätte, Wyoming. Oligocene locality includes the South Dakota School of Mines.
Comments	*Boavus occidentalis* is an extinct species of boiid snake that is primarily known from Eocene Wyoming. It probably lived a lifestyle similar to *Boa constrictor*, stalking and ambushing small vertebrates in rainforest undergrowth and jungle scrub, including birds, lizards, primitive rodents, and possibly even primitive, dog-sized horses. *B. occidentalis* lived with other species of *Boavus*, though, how it interacted with them on an ecological level remains unknown.
	B. occidentalis survives the Eocene-Oligocene boundary, as three vertebrae found in Orellan-aged strata from South Dakota are attributed to it. Another species, *B. affinis*, may possibly have survived into the Late Miocene in Texas.

Name

Harryhausenia galantensis

Phylum	Arthropoda
Subphylum	Crustacea
Class	Malacostraca
Order	Decapoda
Superfamily	Hippoidea
Family	Albuneidae
Subfamily	Albuneinae
Size	Carapace less than 2 centimeters wide or long.
Time Period	Rupellian stage of the Late Oligocene, 32 to 27 million years ago.
Location	Holotype found near Contrá Galanti, Piedmont Basin, near Cassinelle, Liguria region, Italy.
Comments	In 2001, Italian scientists described a fossil sand crab from early Oligocene marine strata in the Piedmont Basin, naming it *"Paralbunea galantensis,"* in reference to how it resembled living members of the living sand crab genus *Paralbunea* (who, today, are found in sandy beachs of the Old World Tropics). In 2004, another study was published noting that *"P."* galantensis had more similarities to another sand crab genus, *Zygopa*, and those researchers then placed it in its own genus, *Harryhausenia*, honoring famed dynamator, Ray Harryhausen, for his enormous contributions for movie monster magic (as well as being a reference to the giant crab monster in the 1961 movie "Mysterious Island").

Although only one carapace is known of *Harryhausenia galantensis*, it lived much like other albuneid sand crabs, burying itself in the sand while using its flattened, fan-like pincer-less first pair of legs, modified from the ancestral pinching chelae, to generate water currents to pull plankton out of the water column and into its mouth and antennae.

Name   *Phorusrhacos longissimus*

Phylum   Chordata

Class   Aves

Order   Cariamiformes

Family   Phorusrhacidae

Subfamily   Phorusrhacinae

Size   Skeletal material suggests an animal up to 2.5 meters tall. Skull up to 60 centimeters long.

Time Period   Colhuehuapian to Laventan land stages, Early to Middle Miocene period, 20 to 13 million years ago.

Location   Santa Cruz and Monte León Formations, Patagonia, Argentina

Comments   *Phorusrhacos longissimus* is probably the best known of all of the "terror birds," an extinct family of mostly South American, mostly flightless birds of prey related to the seriema. It is the type species of Phorusrhacidae. The generic name translates as "wrinkle-bearer," in reference to the wrinkled surfaces on the bones of the jaw: the specific name translates as "very long," in reference to the long mandible.

Phorusrhacos was an apex predator on the Miocene Patagonian savannahs, charging after prey rather than chasing them over long distances. Once within range, the living animal would have subdued prey by kicking and pecking it to death with its powerful, taloned feet, and its massive, ax-like beak. The biomechanics of the beak and jaws show that the animal had a very weak bite force, and most likely used its large, hook-tipped beak to tear flesh from already subdued prey.

Name	*Enhydritherium terraenovae*
Phylum	Chordata
Class	Mammalia
Order	Carnivora
Family	Mustelidae
Subfamily	Lutrinae
Size	Somewhat larger than the modern sea otter.
Time Period	From Middle Hemphillian to Middle Blancan stages, Late Miocene to Middle Pliocene, 9 to 5 million years ago.
Location	Bone Valley Formation, Florida, San Joaquin Formation, California, and Juchipila Basin, Zacatecas, Mexico.
Comments	*Enhydritherium terraenovae* is an extinct species of North American, mostly marine otter ancestral to the modern sea otter, *Enhydra lutris*, representing a transitional form between the sea otter, and the extinct, tropical Asian otter genus *Enhydriodon*. The generic name notes the similarities of the fossil materials with the sea otter, and the specific name refers to how the species is a direct descendant of another fossil otter from the Late Miocene of Spain, which apparently swam across the Atlantic Ocean to Florida, where *E. terraenovae*'s oldest remains are found.
	During the Pliocene, *E. terraenovae* spread along the southern coasts of North America, prior to the formation of the Central American Isthmus, an exodus confirmed by a lone, 6 million year old jawbone found in Pliocene freshwater strata at Zacatecas, Central Mexico. The Zacatecas fossil shows that *E. terraenovae*, unlike its descendant, were able to enter into, if not thrive in freshwater environments.

Name	*Toxodon platensis*
Phylum	Chordata
Class	Mammalia
Order	Notoungulata
Family	Toxodontidae
Subfamily	Toxodontinae
Size	Holotype specimen about 53 millimeters, adult shell lengths ranging from 48 to 55 millimeters
Time Period	Piacenzian to Atlantic land stages, from Late Pliocene to Middle Holocene, 3 million years ago to 5,000 years ago.
Location	Fossils found from Uruguay and Patagonia.
Comments	*Toxodon platensis* is an extinct notoungulate ungulate mammal from the Neogene and Quaternary of Uruguay and Argentina, and is among the last of the notoungulates, having gone extinct when South America was first colonized by humans during the Holocene, long after most other notoungulates went extinct during the Pliocene.

The first fossil of it was a skull found and purchased by Charles Darwin in order to rescue it from some children using it for target practice. At the time, on account of the prominent incisors, Darwin thought it was some sort of giant rodent. Later researchers would understand it to be a massive, herbivorous mammal, and mistakenly assume it was a semi-aquatic analogue to the hippopotamus. Later still, researchers nixed this idea when it was noted that the fossils of *T. platensis* were never found in aquatic strata, and that the nostrils were not at a high point at the skull to keep them out of the water. It and other species of *Toxodon* are now thought to be lumbering browsers that dwelled in arid scrub, analogous to (hornless rhinoceroses).

Samples of collagen taken from Holocene-aged fossils were used in protein analyses, and show that the notoungulates' closest living relatives are the perissodactyls (rhinoceroses, horses and tapirs), with the two groups having diverged at the end of the Cretaceous.

Name

Mekosuchus inexpectans

Phylum Chordata

Class Reptilia

clade Archosauria

Order Crocodilia

Family Crocodylidae

Subfamily Mekosuchinae

Size Estimated to be up to 2 meters long.

Time Period Late Holocene, about 4,000 years ago (~2000 BCE)

Location Subfossils found in the Pindai Grottoes, New Caledonia.

Comments *Mekosuchus inexpectans* is an extinct crocodile from the island of New Caledonia. It went extinct soon after the island was colonized by the ancient Lapita Culture, possibly due to overhunting.

M. inexpectans is one of the last of the Mekosuchinae crocodiles, a subgroup of true crocodiles that evolved and flourished in Australia, only to go into a steep decline during the Pliocene. The genus *Mekosuchus* first appears in the fossil record during the Oligocene of Queensland. Eventually, some time during the Pliocene or Pleistocene, species of *Mekosuchus* would cross the Coral Sea via the now sunken Greater Chesterfield Island before emigrating into Polynesia. This migration would also produce the Fijian genus, *Volia*. Both the Polynesian *Mekosuchus* and *Volia* would perish during the Middle Holocene due to contact and predation by humans from the Lapita Culture. Some figures in New Caledonian Lapita pottery depict *M. inexpectans.*

M. inexpectans preyed on snails, as there is a lack of indigenous large prey to sustain a population of crocodiles (big or small), and *M. inexpectans* had modified back teeth near the posterior of its jaws that would have allowed it to easily crush snail shells with.

Bibliography

- Aguilera, Orangel A., and Alfredo A. Carlini, eds. *Urumaco and Venezuelan paleontology: The fossil record of the Northern Neotropics*. Indiana University Press, 2010.

- Alvarenga, Herculano M. F. & Höfling, Elizabeth (2003): *Systematic revision of the Phorusrhacidae (Aves: Ralliformes). Papéis Avulsos de Zoologia* **43**(4): 55-91

- Arkell, W. J., W. M. Furnish, and Bernhard Kummel. *Treatise on Invertebrate Paleontology, Part L: Mollusca 4, Cephalopoda, Ammonoidea*. Geological Society of America, 1957.

- Amthor, Joachim E., et al. "Extinction of Cloudina and Namacalathus at the Precambrian-Cambrian boundary in Oman." *Geology* 31.5 (2003): 431-434.

- Bartels, Christoph, Derek EG Briggs, and Günther Brassel. *The fossils of the Hunsrück Slate: marine life in the Devonian*. Cambridge University Press, 1998.

- Balouet, J-C., and E. Buffetaut. "Mekosuchus inexpectatus, ng, n. sp., crocodilien nouveau de l'Holocene de Nouvelle Calédonie." *Comptes rendus de l'Académie des sciences. Série 2, Mécanique, Physique, Chimie, Sciences de l'univers, Sciences de la Terre* 304.14 (1987): 853-856.

- Blieck, Alain. "Les Hétérostracés Ptéraspidiformes, Agnathes du Silurien-Dévonien du Continent nord-atlantique et des blocs avoisinants: révision systématique, phylogénie, biostratigraphie, biogéographie." (1984).

- Bockelie, J. FREDRIK. "The Middle Ordovician of the Oslo region, Norway, 30. The eocrinoid genera Cryptocrinites, Rhipidocystis and Bockia." *Norsk Geologisk Tidsskrift* 61 (1981): 123-147.

- Boyko, Christopher B. "A new genus of fossil sand crab (Anomura: Albuneidae) from the Oligocene of Italy." *Palaeontology* 47.4 (2004): 933-936.

- Burrow, Carole J. "A partial articulated acanthodian from the Silurian of New Brunswick, Canada." *Canadian Journal of Earth Sciences* 48.9 (2011): 1329-1341.

- Burrow, Carole J., and David Rudkin. "Oldest near-complete acanthodian: the first vertebrate from the Silurian Bertie Formation Konservat-Lagerstätte, Ontario." *PloS one* 9.8 (2014): e104171.

- Cau, Andrea, et al. "Synchrotron scanning reveals amphibious ecomorphology in a new clade of bird-like dinosaurs." *Nature*552.7685 (2017): 395.

- Chlupáč, I., and V. Havlíček. "Kodymirus ng, a new aglaspid merostome of the Cambrian of Bohemia." *Sborník Geologickych Věd. Paleontologie* 6 (1965): 7-20.

- De Angeli, A., and S. Marangon. "Paralbunea galantensis, nuova specie di anomuro oligocenico del Bacino Ligure-Piemontese (Italia settentrionale)." *Studi Trentini di Scienze Naturali, Acta Geologica* 76.1999 (2001): 99-105.

- EZCuRRA, Martín D. "A review of the systematic position of the dinosauriform archosaur Eucoelophysis baldwini Sullivan & Lucas, 1999 from the Upper Triassic of New Mexico, USA." *Geodiversitas* 28.4 (2006): 649-684.

- Fedonkin, Mikhail A., et al. *The rise of animals: evolution and diversification of the kingdom Animalia*. JHU Press, 2007.

- Fernandez-Lopez, Sixto Rafael. "Lower Bathonian ammonites of Serra de la Creu (Tivissa, Catalan Basin, Spain)." *Revue de Paléobiologie* 19 (2000): 45-52.

- Frickhinger, Karl Albert. *Fossil atlas, fishes*. Mergus, 1995.

- Guanbang, Liu, and Wang Qian. "New material of Sinohelicoprion from Changxing, Zhejiang province." *Vertebr. PalAsiatica* 32.4 (1994): 244-248.

- Gilmore, Charles W. *Fossil snakes of North America.* Vol. 9. Geological Society of America, 1938.

- Harrington, H. J. "General description of Trilobita." *Treatise on invertebrate paleontology, Part O, Arthropoda* 1 (1959): 38-117.

- Holman, J. Alan (2000). Fossil Snakes of North America: Origin, Evolution, Distribution, Paleoecology. Indiana University Press. pp. 357 (pp 40-49). ISBN 9780253337214.

- Hou Xian-Guang (1999). "New rare bivalved arthropods from the Lower Cambrian Chengjiang Fauna, Yunnan, China". *Journal of Paleontology.* **73**(1): 102–116.

- KONDRASHOV, PETER E., and SPENCER G. LUCAS. "PALEOCENE VERTEBRATE FAUNAS OF THE SAN JUAN BASIN, NEW MEXICO." *Vertebrate Paleontology in New Mexico: Bulletin 68* 68: 131.

- Lambert, W. David. "The osteology and paleoecology of the giant otter Enhydritherium terraenovae." *Journal of Vertebrate Paleontology* 17.4 (1997): 738-749.

- Lindsay, Everett H., Louis L. Jacobs, and Robert F. Butler. "Biostratigraphy and magnetostratigraphy of Paleocene terrestrial deposits, San Juan Basin, New Mexico." *Geology*6.7 (1978): 425-429.

- Lundberg, John G., et al. "Discovery of African roots for the Mesoamerican Chiapas catfish, Lacantunia enigmatica, requires an ancient intercontinental passage." *Proceedings of the Academy of Natural Sciences of Philadelphia* 156.1 (2007): 39-54.

- Mead, Jim I., et al. "New extinct mekosuchine crocodile from Vanuatu, South Pacific." *Copeia* 2002.3 (2002): 632-641.

- Molnar, R. E., T. Worthy, and P. M. A. Willis. "An extinct Pleistocene endemic mekosuchine crocodylian from Fiji." *Journal of Vertebrate Paleontology* 22.3 (2002): 612-628.

- Page, K. N. "Observations on the succession of ammonite faunas in the Bathonian (Middle Jurassic) of south-west England, and their correlation with Sub-MediterraneanStandard Zonation'." *PROCEEDINGS-USSHER SOCIETY* 9 (1996): 045-053.

- Petuch, Edward J. *Cenozoic seas: the view from eastern North America.* CRC Press, 2003.

- Prothero, Donald R., and Scott E. Foss, eds. *The evolution of artiodactyls.* JHU Press, 2007.

- Rozhnov, S.V. and Kushlina, V.B. 1994. Interpretation of new data on *Bolboporites* Pander, 1830 (Echinodermata; Ordovician), p. 179-180, in David, B., Guille, A., Féral, J.-P. & Roux, M. (eds.), Echinoderms through time (Balkema, Rotterdam).

- Schweigert, Günter, and Volker Dietze. *Revision der dimorphen Ammonitengattungen Phlycticeras Hyatt-Oecoptychius Neumayr (Strigoceratidae, Mitteljura).* Staatl. Museum für Naturkunde, 1998.

- Schweitzer, Carrie E., et al. "New crabs from the Eocene and Oligocene of Baja California Sur, Mexico and an assessment of the evolutionary and paleobiogeographic implications of Mexican fossil decapods." *Journal of Paleontology* 76.sp59 (2002): 1-44.

- Szalay, Frederick S., and Stephen Jay Gould. "Asiatic Mesonychidae (Mammalia, Condylarthra). Bulletin of the AMNH; v. 132, article 2." (1966).

- Tseng, Z. Jack, et al. "Discovery of the fossil otter Enhydritherium terraenovae (Carnivora, Mammalia) in Mexico reconciles a palaeozoogeographic mystery." *Biology letters*13.6 (2017): 20170259.

- Turner, Alan. *National Geographic Prehistoric Mammals.* National Geographic, 2004.

- Weller, J. Marvin. "Carboniferous trilobite genera." *Journal of Paleontology* (1936): 704-714.

About the Artist

Stanton F. Fink is a student of Biology and Chinese Medicine, and makes a hobby of drawing monsters and researching flowers, arcane-looking creatures, prehistoric animals, fish, reptiles, birds and the occasional, really grotesque fungal fruiting body.

Stanton grew up and went to school in California and is currently living, drawing, and gardening in Oregon.